Hi. I'm Jess Wood, but you can call me Woody. Thanks for reading my book. It shows you've got good taste! This all started out as a Year 9 topic at school. Mr Lee, our teacher, said we could choose the thing we liked best. For me, that was a no-brainer. Girls' football.

I play it.

I watch it.

I live it.

I love it.

And now I'm writing about it. Get in!

Girls rule

Just so you know:

- ☺ When I say girls' football, I mean 8 to 17 year olds. After that, it's women's or ladies' football. (Although my dad says I'll never be a lady the way I clomp round the house. Ha, ha.)

- ☺ Girls' football follows the same FA rules as boys' football.

- ☺ FA stands for Football Association.

- ☺ Every country has its own FA. I live in North Wales, so my FA is FAW. What's yours?

- ☺ FIFA is the body that governs all the FAs in different countries of the world.

Go Wales

Woody

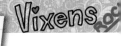

Born kicking

I thought I'd start by telling you how I got into football. Basically, I didn't have much choice. My family are all football fanatics. Mum is Welsh, so I support Wales. Dad is English, so I follow his club, Everton. We follow Everton Ladies, too. We go to as many matches as we can.

I started playing at junior school. It was a mixed team, boys and girls. I was the goalie. Wahoo!

I was gutted when I got to high school and found I couldn't carry on. There wasn't a girls' team and I couldn't join the boys' one because in Wales you can only play mixed football until you are 12.

England isn't much better – their age limit is 13. In Scotland and Northern Ireland, I could have played until I was 15. In fact, in Northern Ireland they encourage mixed football for as long as possible.

Check out this mixed game in Northern Ireland!

Go Wales

Woody

Other countries such as Sweden and Norway don't even have an age limit. They are like Northern Ireland and feel it benefits girls to play with boys. It makes them tougher.

The Welsh and English FAs disagree. They reckon our physical development is too different by the age of 13 and we need separate training.

Still, it worked out OK for me in the end. I joined the Vixens, a grassroots team near where I live. Grassroots means it's not attached to a major league club and is run by volunteers (usually parents). It has a good level of training though.

Teams that do well can progress from local leagues to premier league level. This is the same for boys and girls.

Girls rule

England U15/U17 Squad

↑

FA Elite Performance Camps

↑

FA Girls' Centre of Excellence

↑

FA Player Development Centre

↑

Local Grassroots Football

*According to She Kicks®
magazine, this is how you
move up in the world.*

Go Wales

Woody

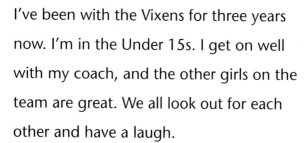

I've been with the Vixens for three years now. I'm in the Under 15s. I get on well with my coach, and the other girls on the team are great. We all look out for each other and have a laugh.

My dream is to play in goal for Wales. To make that dream come true I'd have to follow what is called a **player pathway**. It goes something like this:

A **Player Observer Volunteer** (or scout) comes to watch me.

I dazzle them so much I get sent to a **regional camp** for additional training.

Girls rule

Some lucky girls being trained by a player from Chelsea Ladies FC.

After that I'm invited to attend a **Girls' Performance Centre**. (Wales has three.) The centres are where top class coaches train the U15 and U17 national squads. They are held three or four times a season and usually last a few days. Football with sleepovers – wicked!

I thought I'd better find out how girls in other countries get into football, in case Wales is unusual or something.

It turns out Scotland and Northern Ireland have similar setups. Schools, summer festivals and programmes are all different ways in which girls there become involved.

It's the same in England, except for the most talented players. They can either stay with their grassroots team and have extra support like us, or …

… go to a **Centre of Excellence** (COE). A Centre of Excellence is like a boy's academy and is linked to an FA league club.

Girls rule

GOA

☺ There are 31 FA Girls' COEs in England.

☺ Each age group averages 18 in a squad.

☺ They're only allowed to play other COEs in their region so that they get used to playing at a certain level.

Go Wales

Quick feet, girls! These are the Under 17s for Chelsea and Arsenal, battling it out at the COE final.

Woody

Two 13 year olds, Courtney Limb and Olivia Leslie, attend Lincoln City Ladies' Centre of Excellence. They were both nine when they were spotted playing for their local mixed teams and invited to go for a trial.

Courtney, a striker, describes what happened.

Girls rule

GOA

I went to dance classes when I was three, but when I started school I discovered kicking a ball around at playtimes was more my thing. One of the boys' dads suggested I join a local team called East Coast Juniors.

I played for them for three or four years. I was the only girl and the opposing boys' teams would sometimes make fun of me. They soon stopped when I tackled them, though. They didn't call me the Terminator for nothing! Then, when I was nine, I was spotted by the manager of Lincoln City's Centre of Excellence and invited to go for a trial …

Go Wales

Here's Courtney the Terminator in action.

Nice ball control there, Olivia.

Woody

… *I was so nervous. There were 150 girls at my first trial and 80 at the second. The trials were held in a big school gym and I remember feeling lonely because I didn't know anyone. I couldn't believe it when I got in, especially with being a diabetic.*

Olivia was really nervous at her trial, too.

It was scary, especially when a woman went round with a clipboard taking notes. They sent a letter about a week later. When I told my friend Georgia I'd got in, she gave me a piggyback down the street to celebrate!

So that's the UK, but what about the rest of the world? Well here's something to get your head round.

An incredible 29 million women and girls play football worldwide.

Wow! Girls play even in countries not known for football.

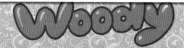

Juhi

Juhi lives in India. She is 18 and a student. She plays midfield for Bodyline FC and has represented her state eight times. Here's what she says.

> Hi. My name is Juhi Shah and I live in Mumbai. I love sport. It has always been in my blood. When I was little I was good at athletics, but we moved house when I was nine. At my new school I started playing football instead …

Girls rule

GOA

… I got a buzz out of doing slide tackles. I got a buzz out of being part of a team, too. It was unusual to see girls play football when I was young. People thought it was only for boys, but that made me want to play it even more.

Luckily my family and my school supported me. I played at high school and I now play for my university as well as Bodyline FC.

Go Wales

Woody

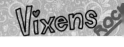

**FIFA has
135 women's teams
and
205 men's teams**

At first, I was blown away by how popular girls' football is, because I knew we were fairly new to the game. Everton FC was founded in 1878, for example, but Everton Ladies FC was founded over a hundred years later, in 1983.

You can see from the table opposite that it's a similar story at club level round Europe.

Looking at that, you'd think girls were the new kids on the block, wouldn't you?

Well, you'd be dead wrong.

Girls rule

GOA

Club	Year club founded: Men	Year club founded: Women
Barcelona (Spain)	1899	2001
Glasgow (Scotland)	Rangers 1872	Glasgow City LFC 1998
Arsenal (England)	1886	1987
Frankfurt (Germany)	FSV 1899	FFC 1998
Cardiff (Wales)	City 1899	1975
Glentoran (Northern Ireland)	1882	1987

Go Wales

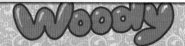

Back in the day

OK, quick history lesson. Football – as in kicking a ball about with your feet – has been around for about 2000 years.

- It has roots in China, Europe and North and South America.

- As far back as 1314, Edward II was moaning that lads were playing football instead of practising archery.

Even in 1680, the ball needed filling with air.

Girls rule

GOA

⚽ Public schools such as Harrow and Eton played the game from the mid-1750s, but each school had different rules. That caused problems when they played each other. In 1848 they met in Cambridge to agree what the rules should be. Amazingly enough, these were known as the Cambridge Rules!

⚽ Sheffield FC is the oldest club (1857). It was their rules the FA used when they started in 1863. The Sheffield FC Rules allowed for more contact in the game than the Cambridge Rules. It was still seen as a "gentleman's" game though.

Some gents playing the Sheffield Rules.

As for the ladies …

☺ Wall paintings showing women playing football have been found in China. They date from around AD 25–220. That's nearly 2000 years ago.

☺ There are reports of ladies' matches between England and Scotland in 1881.

☺ The first known club team, the British Ladies Football Club, was formed in 1895.

That's pretty similar timing, right? So what happened? How come most women's teams today only date back to the 1970s and 80s?

Men, that's what happened.

Girls rule

GOA

They just wouldn't take women seriously. I'm not saying all men. Some were supportive. The British Ladies were trained by a Tottenham Hotspur player, J W Julian, for example. But, by and large, men didn't take kindly to women playing football.

In Scotland, some of the 1881 matches didn't finish because the crowd got angry. The police had to step in and stop the women from being hit. The papers thought these early matches were the "beginning and end for the ladies' game".

Ladies International Match – Scotland v England

A rather novel football match took place on Saturday between teams of lady players representing England and Scotland ...

Glasgow Herald, 1881

Huh. The end – no chance! Not with women like **Nettie Honeyball** around. Nettie was the one who formed the British Ladies Football Club (BLFC). She was all for equal rights. She thought that if women wanted to play football, they should. She said they weren't just "useless ornaments". Go Nettie!

Nettie split the squad into two sides. Although they were all from the London area, one was called "North" and wore red. The other was called "South" and wore light blue. The first time they played, at a ground in Crouch End, London, 10 000 people came to watch. It was a huge event. North won 7–1.

At first, people were only interested in what the team wore. Women weren't supposed to play much sport and if they did it had to be in a "petticoat". A petticoat was like a massive, long underskirt.

Girls rule

Go Wales

The lady herself: Nettie Honeyball

As you can see from the picture opposite, the teams didn't wear petticoats. They wore long-sleeved blouses and baggy knickerbockers. They had heavy leather shin pads strapped over their socks (like men did) and men's boots on their feet. To top it all off, they sometimes wore a cap with a tassel hanging from it. Stylish!

The standard of football was not very good. One newspaper said the ladies "wandered about aimlessly". I think it was amazing they could wander anywhere in that kit.

Between March 1895 and June 1896, the BLFC played 75 matches throughout Britain and Ireland, mainly against each other. Nothing was heard of them after 1896, but Nettie had proved her point.

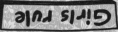

GOA

British Ladies North team (Nettie, second left at the back). Cheer up, ladies! Don't you know you're making history?

The kicking Kerrs

The next time female footballers got noticed was during the First World War (1914–1918). When the men went to fight, the women went to work. A lot of them went to work in munitions factories, making ammunition and weapons. All workers were encouraged to play sport and most factories had a women's football team. The matches raised a lot of money for charity.

Munitions workers, 1914.

Girls rule

GOA

One team, from Preston in Lancashire, became famous.

They were the Dick, Kerr Ladies, named after their factory, Dick, Kerr & Co Ltd.

- ⚽ They were the first women's team to wear shorts.

- ⚽ They were the first to play overseas (in France).

- ⚽ They once played in front of a record crowd of 53 000 (Boxing Day at Everton FC's ground, Goodison Park, in 1920).

The Dick, Kerr Ladies team – undefeated in 1920 and 1921.

The Dick, Kerr left-winger, Lily Parr, was the first woman in the National Football Museum Hall of Fame. In her career she scored over 1000 goals. Probably only Pelé has scored more. What a legend.

Hope there's no one from the FA passing by! Lily Parr aims a javelin during training for the Dick, Kerr team.

When the war ended, women's football was as popular as ever. In fact it was too popular. Guess what the English FA did?

Girls rule

In 1921 they banned women from playing on their grounds. They gave rubbish reasons. They said the money raised for charity wasn't being checked properly.

Then they said:

> "We feel that the game of football is quite unsuitable for females and ought not to be encouraged."

The ban meant teams couldn't play at decent grounds or have proper referees. None of the matches and leagues was seen as "official". In other words, they didn't count.

The FA didn't lift the ban until 1971. That's 50 years later. Gail Newsham, who wrote a book about the Dick, Kerr Ladies, said the ban **"changed the course of the women's game forever"**.

Huh! Just a bit!

Going up, up, up ...

Things have improved loads since then, thank goodness. Although it took a while to catch up with countries such as Sweden and Norway, who didn't have a ban, England is now one of the top women's football-playing countries in the world.

Girls rule

GOA

Germany has had even more success. They were banned for a while, too, but since forming a national squad in 1982, they've won the World Cup twice and European Championships seven times. Their record is almost as good as the USA's.

Did you know?

Germany is the only country to have won the World Cup in both the men's and women's tournaments.

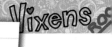

USA! USA!

The USA has dominated women's football since the 1980s.

It seems weird that the USA is such a force because "soccer", as they call it, isn't the major sport there. But maybe that's why the women are so successful. They've never suffered from being compared to the men all the time.

It's the same in countries like China, Japan, Canada, Iceland, North Korea and South Korea. The women's teams there are ranked way higher than the men's.

★ Awesome USA in numbers ★

2 World Cups

4 Olympic gold medals

90 185 fans saw the 1999 FIFA World Cup Final in California: USA v China

Title IX

Another reason for the USA's success is **Title IX**.

Title IX was a law passed in 1972 giving the same educational rights to all. That included rights to sports and sports' funding. It meant female students could be funded to play "soccer" and study at the same time.

Nearly every campus had a team. That led to a better standard of play than elsewhere and a huge pool of talent. The game became more popular and top players were able to make a living out of playing football for the first time.

The USA's Abby Wambach has scored a huge 143 international goals!

VIXENS

EVERTON FC

There are only a lucky few female footballers who earn money. Most don't get a bean, either in the States or elsewhere. Many have to hold down a job, raise families, train midweek and play matches at weekends. That can cause real problems.

In 2010, Glasgow City LFC and Scotland defender Emma Fernon revealed she has lost three jobs because of taking time off to play for Scotland. Some clubs can't even pay travel costs. Can you believe that?

Girls rule

GOA

Juhi can believe it. It's a similar story in India, too. She has friends who dropped out of the college team because they couldn't afford to travel to away matches.

There's very little money in women's football here. My Bodyline coach pays for our kit himself. Also, playing in national tournaments can be difficult because India is so huge. For example, two years ago I was in an Under 17 tournament in Mizoram …

> … *Mizoram is in the far east of India.*
> *We travelled part of the way by train. That took*
> *three days. We didn't have reserved seats and*
> *had to sit near smelly, disgusting bathrooms.*
> *After that was another two-day bus journey.*
> *We had to play the very next day. No wonder we*
> *lost 8–0!*

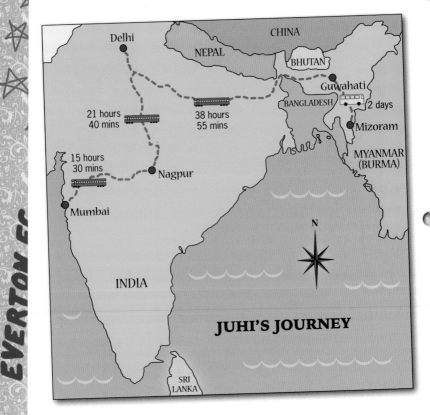

JUHI'S JOURNEY

Emma and Juhi's stories really made me cross. You shouldn't get sacked and you shouldn't have to drop out of football for lack of money. Not when some blokes are on about five million pounds an hour.

I talked to my dad about it. Dad said it was a tricky one.

"Not every footballer is earning megabucks; it's only a few. And all clubs have to raise money, Jess. They do it from ticket sales, TV, sponsorships and transfer deals. The women's game doesn't earn much from these yet, so there's nothing left over to pay wages on top."

"Why don't they charge more for tickets?" I asked.

The reason I mentioned that was because of the difference between what we pay to watch Everton and Everton Ladies. Everton Ladies are in the Women's Super League, so do get paid a bit, but even then they don't charge much for tickets.

Just look at the difference in prices for tickets to watch the men's and women's teams.

Everton FC season 2011–2012

Season ticket (adult) starts at £399.00

Match day ticket (adult) £30–£37.00

Everton Ladies FC season 2011–2012

Season ticket (adult) £22.00

Match day ticket (adult) £4.00

Girls rule

Dad explained they can't charge more. Not until they get people through the turnstiles.

He had a point. When Everton Ladies played Arsenal Ladies (away) in 2011, attendance was 611 – and that's a good turnout.

The men's attendance for their tie with Arsenal? 60 006.

"So why don't fans who support the men's team support the women, too?" I asked.

Dad shrugged. "Some do, but not all women's teams are linked to a men's team like Everton. A lot are independent. Also, men's football is different. It's faster and more physical. You can't compare like-for-like."

"Huh! Maybe you could if we hadn't been banned for fifty years!" I told him.

Did you know?

80 203 tickets were sold for the 2012 Olympic women's football final between the USA and Japan.

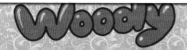

VIXENS

Still, it's not all about money and league tables, is it? For most girls (and boys), that side of football isn't as important as the other things it does. Programmes such as EduSport in Zambia, or Go Sisters World Series, use football to empower girls, raise their self-esteem and teach them about teamwork.

I totally get that. Playing has made me a lot more self-confident. Juhi feels the same. She says that, despite everything, she would never give up football: "I am passionate about it. Women's football is growing all the time in India and I am proud to be part of it".

EVERTON

Girls rule

GOA

Fan-tastic

One thing I would like is more stuff about girls' footy on TV and in magazines. I'd love to read match reports and find out more about my favourite footballers, like Natasha Dowie.

Natasha plays for Everton Ladies ☺ and England ☹. It's her name I have on the back of my shirt. She's amazing. She's a striker, but she always falls back to help her midfield and she never gives up. When Everton got to the FA Cup Final against Arsenal in 2010, it was her goal, deep into extra time, that won it.

She'd be interesting to read about, because she comes from a football family. Her dad, Bob, is a coach and her Uncle Iain played for Northern Ireland.

This is Natasha's Uncle Iain playing in an international friendly against France, in 1999.

When Natasha's not playing football, she likes doing normal things like shopping, hanging out with her mates and listening to music.

She's dead stylish, too, on and off the pitch. I made my dad buy me the same brand of boots as hers.

Girls rule

GOA

Jen O'Neill is someone who is doing her bit to help fans like me. Jen is an ex-Sunderland player and the editor of *She Kicks*® magazine and website. She commentates on important women's matches when they're live on TV or the radio, including in the 2012 Olympics. It's really good to hear a woman doing that as well as men.

Did you know?

1.5 million people watched the 2008 FA Women's Cup Final live on TV.

Women's football was the first sporting event to kick off (ha, ha) the 2012 London Olympics.

The girls with the golden boots

Seeing as Jen O'Neill knows tons about players, I asked her to choose her all-time best football team. I hope nobody ever asks me how you say some of the names (no offence).

 Brazil

 China

 England

 Germany

 Norway

 Sweden

 USA

Girls rule

GOA

4-0   Natasha is cool!

Silke Rottenberg

Carla Overbeck   **Jane Törnqvist**   **Gro Espeseth**

Kristine Lilly   **Malin Moström**   **Maren Meinert**   **Marta**

Michelle Akers

Birgit Prinz   **Mia Hamm**

Go Wales

Subs: Kelly Smith (England)

Sun Wen (China)

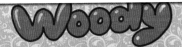

47

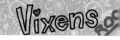

I checked out a few of Jen's players.

Their achievements are incredible.

Birgit Prinz (Germany)

Born: 25 October 1977

Senior playing career: 1992 to 2012

Club teams include: FSV Frankfurt, FFC Frankfurt

Position: Striker

FIFA World Player of the Year: 2003, 2004, 2005.
Runner up: 2007, 2008, 2009, 2010

Birgit Prinz is the most capped European player
(man or woman), with an awesome 214 caps.

A cap is what you get every time you play for your
country. Birgit's caps must have their own room –
there are so many of them.

Marta (Brazil)

Born: 19 Feb 1986

Senior playing career: 2000 to present

Club teams include: Umeå IK, Western New York Flash

Position: Forward

FIFA Women's Player of the Year: 2006 to 2009

Marta comes from a small village in Brazil. When she was 14, her cousin arranged a trial in Rio de Janeiro. It took her three days to get there by bus, alone. When someone asked her if she was scared, she said: "Scared? Why should I be scared? It was in my character to achieve that goal and that was where my goal was."

Go Wales

Sun Wen (China)

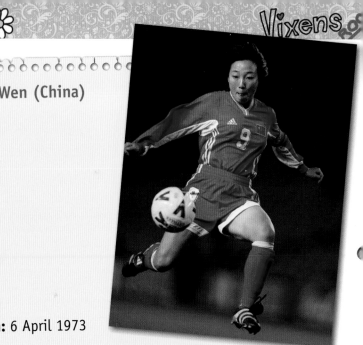

Born: 6 April 1973

Senior playing career: 1989 to 2006

Teams include: Shanghai SVA, Atlanta Beat

Position: Striker

Voted Woman Player of the Century by FIFA in 2002.

When Sun Wen moved to America, she was treated like a superstar by the Chinese community there. The trouble was, she was invited to parties all the time (it is rude to refuse) and fed huge meals until early morning. She ended up falling asleep in training!

Girls rule

GOA

Mia Hamm (USA)

Born: 17 March 1972

Senior playing career:
1982 to 2004

Teams include:
North Carolina Tar Heels
Washington Freedom

Position: Midfield

Mia Hamm has scored more international goals than any man or woman in history. That is amazing, considering she was born with a club foot and spent some of her childhood in a plaster cast. She became so famous in America that Barbie named a doll after her.

Thanks for reading

Well, that's it folks. Time to hand my project in to Mr Lee. I don't know what he'll think of it, but for me it's been life-changing. I never knew so many people had fought so long and so hard to give girls fairer and better opportunities to play football. Every time I pull on my boots from now on, I'll think about that.

I'll think about all the other players round the world pulling on their boots, too.

Here come the girls!

See ya,

Woody
x

Girls rule

GOA

Quiz

Why not check out your national women's team and find out more about them? Have a look at their nicknames, too. My favourite is The Matildas (Australia). Can you guess which names belong to which of the other teams below?

Team	Nickname
England	The Pharoahs
Australia	Blue Yellows
France	The Matildas
Sweden	Samba Queens
Brazil	The Lionesses
Egypt	Banyana Banyana
South Africa	Les Bleues

Answers on page 56

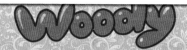

Reader challenge

Word hunt

1 On page 9, find a noun that means "teams".

2 On page 29, find a word that means "abroad".

3 On page 35, find a verb that means "given money".

Text sense

4 What are some of the problems women footballers face because of the lack of money in their sport? (pages 36–39)

5 Other than keeping fit, what are the benefits of playing football? (page 42)

6 Why do you think Woody likes to hear women commentating on football matches? (page 45)

7 Why does Woody find Mia Hamm's achievements so amazing? (page 51)

8 What did Woody learn from doing her project on girls' football? (page 52)

Your views

9. Did you find the book interesting? Did it give you a good understanding of the history of women's football? Give reasons.

10. Do you think women's football should be given the same funding and TV coverage as men's football? Give reasons.

Spell it

With a partner, look at these words and then cover them up.

- perform
- attend
- appear

- performance
- attendance
- appearance

Take it in turns for one of you to read the words aloud. The other person has to try and spell each word. Check your answers, then swap over.

Try it

With a partner, imagine you are preparing to give a talk to a local business person to persuade them to sponsor a new kit for your local girls' football team. Discuss what you would say to persuade them.

William Collins's dream of knowledge for all began with the publication of his first book in 1819. A self-educated mill worker, he not only enriched millions of lives, but also founded a flourishing publishing house. Today, staying true to this spirit, Collins books are packed with inspiration, innovation and practical expertise. They place you at the centre of a world of possibility and give you exactly what you need to explore it.

Collins. Freedom to teach.

Published by Collins Education
An imprint of HarperCollins*Publishers*
77–85 Fulham Palace Road, Hammersmith, London W6 8JB

Browse the complete Collins Education catalogue at **www.collinseducation.com**

Text by Helena Pielichaty
© HarperCollins *Publishers* Limited 2012

Series consultants: Alan Gibbons and Natalie Packer

10 9 8 7 6 5 4 3 2 1
ISBN 978-0-00-746491-3

British Library Cataloguing in Publication Data.
A catalogue record for this publication is available from the British Library.

Commissioned by Catherine Martin

Edited and project-managed by Sue Chapple

Picture research by Grace Glendinning

Design and typesetting by
Jordan Publishing Design Limited

Cover design by Paul Manning

Cover images: (front) Jodie Brett and Amber Gaylor battling during the FA Girls' Youth Cup U17s Centre of Excellence Final. Photo by Jan Kruger – The FA/The FA via Getty Images.
(back) The Dick, Kerr ladies' team circa 1920–1921. Photo by Bob Thomas/Popperfoto/Getty Images.

Quiz answers

England = the Lionesses
France = Les Bleues
Australia = Matildas
South Africa = Banyana Banyana
Sweden = Blue Yellows
Brazil = Samba Queens
Egypt = the Pharaohs

Acknowledgements

From the author:
I wouldn't have been able to write this book without contributions from the following:

Patrick Brennan for information about Nettie Honeyball and the Munitionettes on his website www.donmouth.co.uk; Gail J Newsham: *In A League of their Own*, (Pride of Place Publishing, 1994) and www.dickkerrladies.co.uk; Jen O'Neill of *She Kicks*® magazine www.shekicks.net; Dr. Jean Williams, Senior Lecturer at the International Centre for Sports History and Culture at De Montfort University, Leicester; Alfie Wylie, Manager, Northern Ireland Women's teams; Gus Williams Player development co-ordinator Welsh Football Trust; Natasha Dowie, Everton Ladies and England; Megan Harris, player Lincoln City Ladies WFC and coach at Lincoln Ladies COE; Courtney Leslie and Olivia Limb at Lincoln Ladies WFC centre of excellence; Juhi Shah, Bodyline FC; Fiona Campbell, Sponsorship Manager, Friend of EduSport.

Thank you all so, so much.

The publishers would like to thank the students and teachers of the following schools for their help in trialling the Read On series:

Southfields Academy, London; Queensbury School, Queensbury, Bradford; Langham C of E Primary School, Langham, Rutland; Ratton School, Eastbourne, East Sussex; Northfleet School for Girls, North Fleet, Kent; Westergate Community School, Chichester, West Sussex; Bottesford C of E Primary School, Bottesford, Nottinghamshire; Woodfield Academy, Redditch, Worcestershire; St Richard's Catholic College, Bexhill, East Sussex

The publisher would like to thank the following for permission to reproduce pictures in these pages (t = top, b = bottom, c = centre, l = left, r = right):

p 2 & 3 Robert J. Beyers II/Shutterstock, p 4 Robert Pernell/Shutterstock, p 5 Craigavon City v Lurgan Town in the Mid Ulster Youth League. Photo by RicPics and provided courtesy of the Northern Ireland Football Club, p 7 *She Kicks*® magazine cover images provided courtesy of Jen O'Neill, editor, www.shekicks.net. Design of magazine cover by Neil Shand and photo by Ville Vuorinen, pp 8–9 Warren Little/Getty Images, p 11 Jan Kruger - The FA/The FA via Getty Images, pp 12–14 Images provided courtesy of Courtney Leslie and Olivia Limb, p 15 Vatikaki/Shutterstock, pp 16–17 & 37 All photos of Juhi by Kashvi Gidwani, p 18 Harold Cunningham/Getty Images, p 20 & 28 Hulton Archive/Getty Images, p 21 & 30 Bob Thomas/Popperfoto/Getty Images, p 22 Marilyn Shea, 2005, University of Maine at Farmington, p 23 Popperfoto/Getty Images, p 25 & 27 © HEMEDIA/SWNS Group, p 30 B. Marshall/Fox Photos/Getty Images, p 32 Paul Thomas – The FA/The FA via Getty Images, p 33 Bongarts/Getty Images, p 35 Ronald Martinez/Getty Images, p 36 Photo of Emma Fernon provided courtesy of the Glasgow City FC, www.glasgowcityladiesfc.co.uk. Used with permission from photographer Graeme Berry, p 40l Alex Livesey/Getty Images, p 40r & 43 Matt Lewis – The FA/The FA via Getty Images, p 42 Images provided courtesy of Fiona Campbell, p 44 Michael Cooper/Allsport, p 45 Image provided courtesy of Jen O'Neill, p 48 Boris Streubel/Getty Images, p 49 JOHANNES EISELE/AFP/Getty Images, p 50 Adam Pretty/ALLSPORT, p 51t Sean Garnsworthy/Getty Images, p 51b Piotr & Irena Kolasa/Alamy.